HOW DO I LIVE THROUGH GRIEF?

Strength and Hope
in Time of Loss

HAROLD BAUMAN

BARBOUR
PUBLISHING, INC.
Uhrichsville, Ohio

T5-CCN-237

Published by Barbour Publishing, Inc., P. O. Box 719, Uhrichsville, Ohio 44683 http://www.barbourbooks.com

 Member of the
Evangelical Christian
Publishers Association

Printed in the United States of America.

HOW DO I LIVE THROUGH GRIEF?

CONTENTS

INTRODUCTION

When grief overtakes us, the "valley of the shadow" seems very dark and almost endless. Whatever your loss, this book is written to help you understand and bear your grief, and to know that it can be healed.

SORROW COMES
TO EVERYONE

Sooner or later grief comes to everyone. Grief is no respecter of persons. It is an experience that we do not fully understand until we walk through it ourselves.

There are things that we can know ahead of time to help us when we experience grief. These things will also help us to give understanding, encouragement, and comfort to bereaved friends.

Jesus showed this when Mary and Martha lost their brother, Lazarus. The Gospel of John, chapter 11, records how Jesus came to them. He shared their grief in such a way as to be of help.

When someone close is lost, the broken emotional ties leave a deep sense of sorrow and emptiness. These ties can be severed by death or by the sudden rending of a love relationship, as in the break-up of a home or a courtship.

Grief may be involved also in the loss of health, a severe financial or job loss, or in the confession of sin.

The emotional experience following a significant loss, which we call grief, can come in many ways. To deal with grief we need to understand it.

Now a man named Lazarus was sick. He was from Bethany, the village of Mary and her sister Martha. This Mary, whose brother Lazarus now lay sick, was the same one who poured perfume on the Lord and wiped his feet with her hair. So the sisters sent word to Jesus, "Lord, the one you love is sick."

JOHN 11:1–3

STAGE ONE:
SHOCK

What are the experiences someone goes through in suffering grief?

The first reaction is shock.

The death of a loved one may be abrupt, with no warning. Suddenly the news is received, "He is gone."

A wife whose husband was killed in an industrial accident received the news of his death. She fainted. When she came to, she wanted to know what had happened. She was told and again she fainted. This happened five times before she could stand the blow.

If death follows a prolonged illness or

comes as a result of old age, the shock to the family is not nearly so severe, although it is still there. Anticipating the loss, we move partway through the grief experience before the death comes.

But when death comes, the loss is still real and still a shock. We may feel a tightness in the throat, an inner tenseness we cannot understand, an emptiness in the pit of the stomach. We may feel very tired.

At this stage in the grief experience, those who stand by may not know what to say.

The important thing is not to say something. The important thing is just to be there, to share the experience.

The bereaved person wants to talk about the one who has died, to express grief, to accept the "rightness" of grief feelings. He or she needs to find a good listener.

Someone caught in sudden grief may even have feelings of revolt, of not understanding.

"Why did God let this happen to me?" may be the first reaction.

This is natural in the depth of shock.

There is no need to feel guilty for reacting in this way.

STAGE TWO:
NUMBNESS

T he second stage of grief is the experience of numbness.

We feel as though we are partially under
anesthetic. Things do not seem real. We walk
around in a daze, unable to think clearly.

The shock itself numbs us so that we do
not feel everything.

Usually we do not need heavy sedatives.
In fact, heavier sedation than necessary hin-
ders the grief process.

People in this second stage are not in a
position to work their way through the
"Why?", even though they may ask it.

This is not the time to probe for deep

theological answers regarding what has happened. Rather, we can affirm that the loss is a heavy burden, a deep grief, and brings genuine suffering.

Yet as day follows day, we can be sure that God our Father will provide comfort and understanding, as Jesus brought comfort and hope to Mary and Martha in that home in Bethany.

On his arrival, Jesus found that Lazarus had already been in the tomb for four days. Bethany was less than two miles from Jerusalem, and many Jews had come to Martha and Mary to comfort them in the loss of their brother.

When Martha heard that Jesus was coming, she went out to meet him, but Mary stayed at home. "Lord," Martha said to Jesus, "if you had been here, my brother would not have died. But I know that even now God will give you whatever you ask."

Jesus said to her, "Your brother will rise again."

Martha answered, "I know he will rise again in the resurrection at the last day."

Jesus said to her, "I am the resurrection and the life. He who believes in me will live, even though he dies; and whoever lives and believes in me will never die." JOHN 11:17–26

STAGE THREE:
FANTASY AND GUILT

The third step in the grief process is a struggle between fantasy and reality.

Repeatedly, I have heard people in this situation say, "It seems as if he is just away and he will come back."

A boy of seven and a boy of nine were playing with their father on the living room floor, just a month after their mother had died. In their play, as often happens, the father accidentally hurt the younger boy. Without thinking, the little boy cried out for his mother to come "and make Daddy stop."

In the silence that followed, they all realized that she was not there. The boy's mind was still moving between fantasy and reality.

This experience is normal for a bereaved person, especially when the grief has come suddenly.

This stage is difficult. There is deep emotional attachment to the one who has died. There are experiences associated with his or her memory.

Following the funeral of a young daughter, the father and mother did not touch her room. They left it as it was for a year, and then two years. Still grieving, they heard a sermon which helped them to see that the grief coming from the death of a loved one can be accepted.

One does not have to dry-clean the clothes of the one who has died and put them in the closet, for fear of being disloyal. Rather, the things he or she loved can be used and shared with others.

This understanding can help to resolve the struggle between fantasy and reality.

During this period there may be some

guilt feelings. The grieving person may say, "If only we had tried a different doctor." Or, "If only we had taken her to another hospital, then it would not have happened."

Guilt feelings like these are also a normal part of the grief process. We need not be surprised at them.

However, if real grounds for guilt feelings exist because of resentments or interpersonal injuries that preceded the death, these ought to be dealt with. If they are ignored, such guilt feelings may erupt in critical attitudes towards the other members of the family.

But if guilt feelings are only a reaction of grief, a feeling of somehow being responsible for the loss, then this can be recognized.

We should come to understand that we do not need to feel guilty, as though we had betrayed the person who died.

STAGE FOUR:
RELEASE OF GRIEF

The fourth step in the experience of grief is a release, an utter flood of grief.

This is not to say that grief hasn't already come. Grief will be expressed in each of these stages. But when the person moves to accept the reality of the loss, then their emotions may seem to be let loose.

This also is natural. A sorrowing person should not try to hold back his or her emotions.

This does not mean becoming hysterical or losing control. It means that to shed tears is a normal and often necessary part of the healing process.

It helps us to accept what has happened to the loved one.

We are tempted to try to counteract these emotions by saying, "Brace up—don't cry." A boy whose father died was crying. Someone said, "Now come on, be a man: Grown men don't cry."

This is not realistic. We do shed tears. Jesus cried. He showed His grief. The experience of releasing grief is necessary. Emotions ought not to be pent up inside or there will be an explosion. The release of this pressure may create new problems.

The release of emotions results in cleansing and healing of the person as the grief is shared.

A young man's wife was found to have cancer. The doctor said she had six months to live.

After the operation, the doctor revised the time to three months. The young man prayed that if God would spare his wife for one year, he would give his life to do anything God asked.

His wife lived eleven months, and he felt his prayer was answered. He went through the grief experience composed. He was seemingly happy in his relationship with God.

Some time later he remarried, but he began to feel cold spiritually. His relationship with his second wife was fine, but something was wrong. Two years later, he sat down with his pastor, and began to pour out his heart and the feelings that were down underneath.

Suddenly a whole rush of suppressed emotions broke out, and he cried like a child. Only then did he find healing.

Emotions, when they come, should not be fought. They should not run rampant, but they are a legitimate expression of our feelings. Jesus wept with the two sisters of Lazarus.

[Martha]. . .called her sister Mary aside. "The Teacher is here," she said, "and is asking for you." When Mary heard this, she got up quickly and went to him. Now Jesus had not yet entered the village, but was still at the place where Martha had met him. When the Jews who had been with Mary in the house, comforting her, noticed how quickly she got up and went out, they followed her, supposing she was going to the tomb to mourn there.

*When Mary reached the place
where Jesus was and saw him,
she fell at his feet and said, "Lord,
if you had been here, my brother
would not have died."*

*When Jesus saw her weeping,
and the Jews who had come along
with her also weeping, he was
deeply moved in spirit and trou-
bled. "Where have you laid him?"
he asked.*

*"Come and see, Lord," they
replied.*

*Jesus wept. Then the Jews
said, "See how he loved him!"*

JOHN 11:28–36

STAGE FIVE:
PAINFUL MEMORIES

The fifth step in the grief process is to work through our memories of the one who has died.

This will take longer than the few days from the time of death to the funeral.

It may take months.

We go to church, and the seat beside us is vacant. We walk down the street and see someone who was a close friend of the loved one. Pain strikes again. These memories have to be recognized and accepted.

We need to find someone who will share and listen to our grief in a sympathetic and understanding way. It is healthy to talk openly about our grief from time to time over a period of weeks. It is healthy to express our feelings. This is one way to work it through.

Grief's work is slow. It takes time and involves pain to deal with these memories. This is grief's way.

We are tempted to cherish only the best memories of the one who has died until he or she almost becomes an idol. If we recall less happy memories along with the more pleasant ones, our thoughts of the person are more realistic and truer to human experience.

In accepting the pain and readjusting to living without the person, we need to face and deal with our memories.

It helps to share these with people we can trust.

STAGE SIX:
LEARNING TO
LIVE AGAIN

After we have moved through the experiences described so far, we are ready for the final phase of grief's work: reaffirming life.

When the loss has been accepted, the grief has been spent, and the memories no longer bring unbearable pain, then we can experience a new life.

When someone dies, a part of the one left behind goes with him or her. Losing a loved one is like having a limb amputated.

Acknowledging and accepting this reality is a doorway. Beyond lies a new life.

We may gain new understanding of God's will and purpose for us. We may begin to appreciate in a new way how much God loves and cares for us.

But we ought to guard against hasty, compulsive actions.

When someone dies or is dying, in the heat of our emotions we may be tempted to make a vow, saying we will do this or that.

No, the decisions God seeks are better made in prayer and reflection and, in the case of grief, after the grief work is nearly completed.

A woman lost her son when he was only seven. She vowed that she would walk up the hill to the city graveyard every day to look at his grave. She kept this up until she was an old lady. She had children and grandchildren, but each day she would give several hours to this walk.

Onlookers said, "What devotion!" But this lady was making an idol of her son.

She had not let him go.

Instead of devoting her life to her living children and grandchildren who needed her desperately, she was still expending her emotional energy on one who could no longer profit from her attention. Hanging on to her grief, she did not experience rebirth to a new life.

Many people, after working through the grief process, come to reaffirm life. They invest their lives in a new family or in new work and responsibilities. They begin to live again with purpose.

These six experiences—the sudden shock, the numbness, the struggle between fantasy and reality, the release of grief, the work with memories, and finally the renewal of life—make up the grief process.

WHAT TO TELL
YOUNG CHILDREN

One of the most difficult problems at the time of a death is what to tell young children.

How can they understand the death of a mother or a father, a grandparent or a loved one? Perhaps we have so much difficulty in telling them because we have trouble accepting death ourselves.

Only when we do not fear death ourselves can we communicate trust and confidence to our children.

Our children can understand that God has prepared a home for those who love Him. We do not say to a little daughter,

"God needed your mother more than you did," or she may feel bitter toward God. Rather we say, "Your mother is with God. And some day, when we die, we will go to be with her."

As one mother was telling her son about his grandfather's death, she began to cry. The boy asked, "Mother, why are you crying?"

She replied, "Because we loved Grandpa so much."

After a pause he responded, "When you go, I want to go with you." The son had caught something of the love, the trust, and the faith that it takes to face the experience of death.

Just as children are no longer shut out of the mystery of birth, so they should not be shut out of the mystery of death.

Since children tend to think of death as abandonment, with resulting fears, resentments and loneliness, they should not be further abandoned by being sent off to some distant relative.

34

Though the attempt to protect our children may be motivated by the best intentions, it may result in distorting their emotional experience.

Their greatest need is for reassurance that they will be cared for and loved by those nearest to them.

At the appropriate time and place, we should carefully share information surrounding a death with the children. We should support them in their grief with love and faith.

ACCEPTING DEATH

A number of factors condition the kind of grief experience each of us may have and the grief work which accompanies it.

One factor is our community's expectations and practices in the time of grief.

In the account of Lazarus' death in chapter 11 of John's Gospel, we read that many of the Jews came to Mary and Martha to console them.

Today, we have certain patterns of sharing grief, too.

One custom is to go to the home of the bereaved person. This is much better than sending a card, although a card can very well be sent. Just a handshake or an embrace and whatever brief word we may share will mean much more than something sent from a distance.

By facing together the reality of death and our hopes for the future, we can support each other in the presence of grief.

Another factor that conditions our grief experience is our attitude toward death. If we feel that death is a mistake that ought not to happen, this will tend to make our grief unreal.

We need to realize that death does come. It is not a mistake. Death comes because we are part of an earthly order in which bodies get old and die.

Furthermore, we are finite. We possess limitations. A person drives along the road, does not see the train and is fatally injured. We can struggle a long time over the question, "Was this the will of God?" Or we may choose to believe that God permits human finiteness and limitations to take their course without miraculously intervening.

We can face the reality of death in a helpful way.

Today, the trend is to soften this reality through softening the words we use ("the departed," "passed away") and through funeral practices that tend to play down death.

Actually to see the body before or at the funeral service often helps the healing process to begin.

Our view of death must include, as Jesus' did, the knowledge that the inner person does not die, but goes to his or her eternal reward.

The physical body of the person we loved is now cold, and we suffer loss and grief. But if that person entrusted the future to God, then we can know that he or she is with Him. We experience grief at our loss, yet joy that our loved one is at peace. We sorrow, but not as those who have no hope. We have the confident hope that Jesus gave to His friends at Bethany.

A third factor that conditions the grief

work is the strength of our relationship with the person who died. If we were close to him or her, the experience will be severe, as it was for Mary and Martha. If we were not so close, the experience will be less severe.

ADJUSTING
TAKES TIME

A nother factor that affects the grief experience is how the person died.

If the death is sudden, it comes as a severe shock. If it is anticipated, we may have worked partway through the grief experience before the death occurs. This is something we need to understand.

A young husband may know for months that his wife is suffering from a terminal illness.

Each time he takes her to the doctor he enters deeper into the grief experience.

Each time they go to the hospital he leaves a part of himself behind. By the time she dies, he is already partway through the grief experience, and perhaps a few months later he seems to have fully recovered and come to a new affirmation of life.

Some people may wonder, in such a case, why the husband does not show more grief. It seemingly did not take him long to adjust to the death.

But he has been adjusting all along, having begun much earlier than the community. If he shows interest in finding a new mother for his children, a new companion for himself, this need not be interpreted as not loving his first wife. Rather, he has worked through the grief and has come out a new person ready to reaffirm life.

The manner of death makes a great deal of difference as to how severe the grief experience will be after the death occurs.

Even so, whenever and however the loss comes, the grief is still real.

DEATH IS NOT
THE END

Our experience of grief will also be conditioned by how much the resources of the Christian faith are ours.

The Christian knows that death is not the end, even for the body.

Those who die as Christians will be raised with new and glorious bodies like Jesus' resurrection body. Belief in the resurrection helps us to think of the person as we knew him or her. In addition, it makes us treat the body with respect.

The Christian knows that death is not the end for the inner person.

The spirit of one who has died "in

Christ" does not die, but rather goes to be with Jesus, which the apostle Paul says "is far better."

What is more, the living Christ stays with each grieving believer. As He came to be with Mary and Martha, so He will stay with us to help and comfort. We are not left alone.

In *The Pilgrim's Progress*, Christian and Hopeful come to the river of death. They notice how deep, how wide, how swift it is, and they are afraid.

Suddenly, two men with shining faces and clothes stand beside them. Christian and Hopeful inquire if there is a boat or bridge they can use to cross the river. The two men reply that there is no other way to the gate than through the river. When asked how deep the water is, the strangers say, "You shall find it deeper or shallower as you believe in the King."

All who have faith in Jesus Christ can be strengthened by His presence. He helps them to deal with grief and, when the time comes, to face death itself.

The final resource for the Christian is the support of fellow believers, standing by one another and encouraging one another. Sharing a meal is another expression of fellowship. One family said, "We never imagined how much this could mean until we went through it."

Sharing pulls people together as they stand awed by the experience of death.

The privilege of loving another person deeply involves the risk of separation. We cannot love richly without facing this risk. It is one of life's unchangeables. But though the parting is real and painful, we can count on the resources available to us in Jesus, to help us as grief does its slow work.

The resurrection of Christ can be a reality entered into by those who have physically died. And it can also be a sign of hope for those who have suffered bereavement. With Jesus' help our life can be renewed and deep grief can give way to quiet acceptance and hope.

We know that at our own death, if we belong to Christ, we will share Christ's resurrection and be united once more with those we have lost.

Jesus said to [Martha], "I am the resurrection and the life. He who believes in me will live, even though he dies; and whoever lives and believes in me will never die. Do you believe this?"

Jesus. . .came to the tomb. It was a cave with a stone laid across the entrance. "Take away the stone," he said. . . . They took away the stone. Then Jesus looked up and said, "Father, I thank you that you have heard me. I knew that you always hear me, but I said this for the benefit of the people standing here, that they may believe that you sent me."

When he had said this, Jesus called in a loud voice, "Lazarus, come out!" The dead man came out, his hands and feet wrapped with strips of linen, and a cloth around his face. Jesus said to them, "Take off the grave clothes and let him go."

JOHN 11:25–26, 38, 41–44

Inspirational Library

Beautiful purse/pocket-size editions of Christian classics bound in flexible leatherette. These books make thoughtful gifts for everyone on your list, including yourself!

When I'm on My Knees   The highly popular collection of devotional thoughts on prayer, especially for women.
> Flexible Leatherette $4.97

The Bible Promise Book   Over 1,000 promises from God's Word arranged by topic. What does God promise about matters like: Anger, Illness, Jealousy, Love, Money, Old Age, and Mercy? Find out in this book!
> Flexible Leatherette $3.97

Daily Wisdom for Women   A daily devotional for women seeking biblical wisdom to apply to their lives. Scripture taken from the New American Standard Version of the Bible.
> Flexible Leatherette $4.97

My Daily Prayer Journal   Each page is dated and features a Scripture verse and ample room for you to record your thoughts, prayers, and praises. One page for each day of the year.
> Flexible Leatherette $4.97

Available wherever books are sold.
Or order from:

Barbour Publishing, Inc.
P.O. Box 719
Uhrichsville, OH 44683
http://www.barbourbooks.com

If you order by mail, add $2.00 to your order for shipping.
Prices are subject to change without notice.